EALING TO SLOUGH
including the Heathrow Branch

Vic Mitchell and Keith Smith

MP Middleton Press

Cover picture: Southall depot provided much of the motive power for the route and was amongst the first to house diesel railcars. From left to right on 14th June 1958 are nos 9469, 2224, W30W and 5333. (H.C.Casserley)

Published April 2000

ISBN 1 901706 42 7

© Middleton Press, 2000

Design Deborah Esher
Typesetting Barbara Mitchell

Published by
>   *Middleton Press*
>   *Easebourne Lane*
>   *Midhurst, West Sussex*
>   *GU29 9AZ*
Tel: 01730 813169
Fax: 01730 812601

Printed & bound by Biddles Ltd,
>   *Guildford and Kings Lynn*

CONTENTS

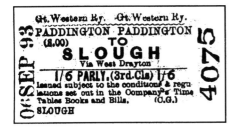
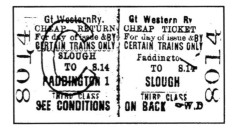

ACKNOWLEDGEMENTS

We are very grateful for the help received from so many of the photographers. Our thanks also go to R.M.Casserley, G.Croughton, R.Instone, N.Langridge, Mr D. and Dr S.Salter, E.Youldon and our ever supportive wives.

I.   The route diagram between 1924, when Iver opened, and 1942, when Brentford closed to passengers. The 1998 Heathrow branch has been added. (J.C.Gillham)

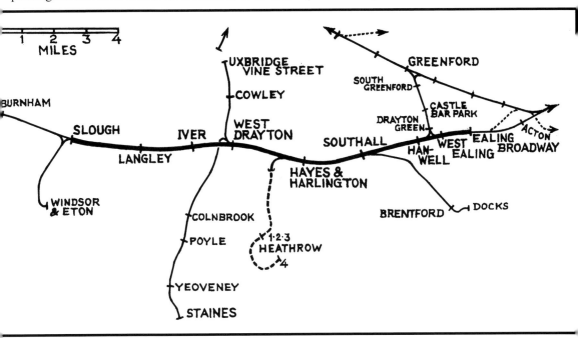

GEOGRAPHICAL SETTING

The whole route lies within the Lower Thames Valley, which was entirely agricultural when the line was built, but it later became extensively urbanised westwards. Three significant Thames tributaries are crossed: the River Brent, near Hanwell, and the River Colne and the Colne Brook, west of West Drayton.

The railway is in close proximity to the Slough branch of the Grand Union Canal between West Drayton and Slough. It passes over the Paddington section of that canal east of Hayes. The canal was so named in 1929, following the amalgamation of a number of waterways.

The Ordnance Survey maps are at 25ins to 1 mile and our journey proceeds from right to left across each one.

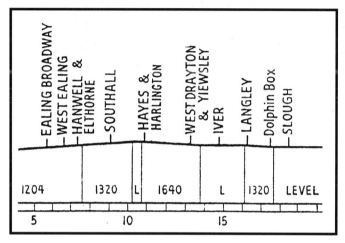

II. Gradient profile with miles from Paddington shown at the bottom.

HISTORICAL BACKGROUND

The first section of the Great Western Railway's London to Bristol line was opened between Paddington and Maidenhead on 4th June 1838, although these stations were some distance from the present ones. The Act for most of the route had been passed on 31st August 1835. Two broad gauge tracks (7ft 0¼ins) were laid and a third one was added east of West Drayton in 1861.

The branch from Slough to Windsor opened on 8th October 1849, with West Drayton to Uxbridge following on 8th September 1856, Southall to Brentford on 18th July 1859, West Drayton to Colnbrook on 9th August 1884 (Staines in 1885) and West Ealing to Greenford on 3rd June 1903.

The quadrupling of the tracks was undertaken in stages, the new pair being laid to standard gauge. The lines through Ealing to Southall were completed on 1st October 1877, Southall to West Drayton followed on 1st June 1879 and the section to Slough came into use on 8th September 1884. A third rail was laid inside much of the broad gauge track to accommodate standard gauge trains; final broad gauge trains ran on 20th May 1892.

There were no major changes until the GWR was nationalised in 1948, to become the Western Region of British Railways, when the visible changes were few. Trains began to appear in sector liveries - InterCity and Network

SouthEast - in the mid-1980s - these being followed in the mid-1990s by Thames Trains and Great Western Trains colours as a prelude to privatisation. The former franchise was let on 13th October 1996 and the latter on 4th February of the same year; the owning companies became

Victory Railway Holdings and First Group respectively.

Heathrow Express began operating its trains between Paddington and Heathrow Junction on 19th January 1998, the branch to Terminal 4 coming into use on 25th May 1998.

The Times announcement on 2nd June 1838.

PASSENGER SERVICES

Initially the company tried to operate eight trains each way on weekdays and six on Sundays, but locomotive reliability was low. The 1850 down timetable showed eleven weekday trains between London and Slough, all but three calling at most stations. There were still six on Sundays.

The 1870 Bradshaw indicated three non-stop trains from Paddington to Slough, one semifast and 15 calling at most stations. There were also eight from Victoria to Southall (or beyond), this service having started in 1863. On Sundays

there were ten from Paddington and three from Victoria. Also starting in 1863 was a service from the City over the Metropolitan Railway. By 1870, two of these ran to Southall and seven continued to Slough and Windsor. GWR trains ceased running from Victoria in 1915 and from the City in 1939.

With the development of the suburbs, train frequency increased and stopping patterns altered, but to list them in detail would make tedious reading.

EALING BROADWAY

III.   The 1875 survey shows the station, with its one short siding, situated in rural surroundings on the edge of the small country town. This station was swept away when the two extra tracks were laid on the north side of the others in 1877. It had opened on 1st December 1838, almost six months after the route itself.

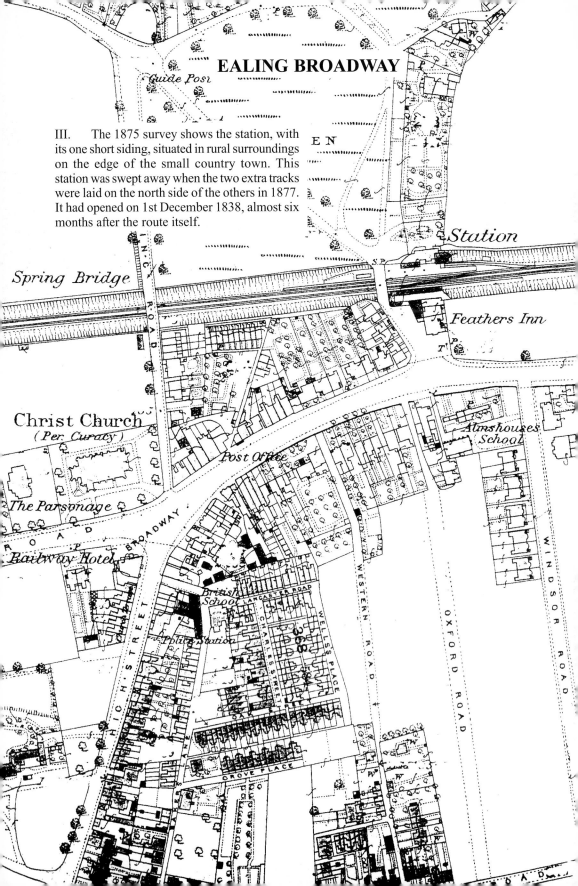

1.   An eastward view includes the new relief lines on the left and the frontage of the second building, which faced the widened road. The earlier and wider brick arch can be seen on the right. A down local train is departing in the Edwardian era. (Lens of Sutton)

2.   The up local platform was well provided with weather protection, seats and advertisements, some of the latter even appearing below the platform edge. The suffix "Broadway" was added in 1875. (Lens of Sutton)

3. Looking west in 1919, we see the original route on the left and a van train on the down relief line. This includes milk vans and thus probably empty milk churns returning to the West Country. (LGRP/NRM)

4. A railmotor from Greenford ends its journey at the up relief platform, while a Central Line train terminates sometime in the 1950s. These trains had been running over the GWR's Ealing & Shepherds Bush Railway since 1920; that line's signal box is visible right of centre. Beyond it is the 1879 District Railway station, which first received electric trains in 1905. (Lens of Sutton)

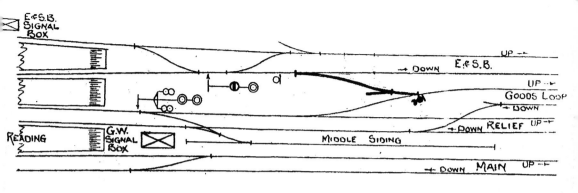

IV. The "Middle siding" was added in 1932 for the layover of Greenford trains and removed in about 1992. The diagram is from October 1945 and highlights a new connection made at that time. The GWR box had 39 levers until then. The "E&S.B." passed to London Transport on 1st January 1948.

5. An up stopping train was hauled by class 9400 0-6-0PT no. 9415 of Slough Shed on 21st May 1960. The footbridge had been added in 1920 to connect all nine platforms and good weather protection was provided. (T.Wright)

6. The exterior was photographed on 27th November 1960, a few days before most of the building was demolished to permit bridge rebuilding. The DR terminus is visible on the left. (J.C.Gillham)

7. No. 6960 *Raveningham Hall* is about to stop at the down main platform with a train for Didcot in misty weather on 26th March 1960. This locomotive, which is now preserved on the Severn Valley Railway, is about to pass over the ATC (Automatic Train Control) ramp. (D.Trevor Rowe)

8.   Another 1960 photograph and this features the 1920 footbridge and 0-6-0PT no. 9409 running through on the down relief line. It will soon pass the site of the 1927 Longfield Avenue signal box, which had 24 levers and closed on 20th March 1955. (J.C.Gillham)

9.   The 65-lever Ealing Broadway box closed on the same day and had been situated in the centre of this eastward view. No. 47183 is approaching with a down oil train on 11th August 1980. The junction indicator on the left had become redundant on 17th September 1972, when the connection to the up goods loop was taken out of use. (D.H.Mitchell)

10.   A few minutes later, parcels car no. W55992 was recorded with two vans in tow at the same location. The middle siding is evident, beyond the hut; it was little used after Greenford services were extended to Paddington. (D.H.Mitchell)

11.   The south side of the station was completely rebuilt in 1963-68 and the 1920 footbridge was removed. A new booking hall was created at the bottom of the office block, but down passengers were given minimal shelter (left). Diesel-electric no. 210002 was working from Reading to Paddington on 29th December 1983. (P.G.Barnes)

12.   Following the Ladbroke Grove disaster on 5th October 1999, Paddington was closed for 16 days and trains terminated here or at Reading. The normally deserted platform 1 was packed with frustrated passengers on the following Saturday as no. 332014 was about to leave, almost empty, for Heathrow Airport at 11.00. This shuttle arrangement was soon withdrawn, but some HSTs started their journeys west from this platform. (V.Mitchell)

Details of the rebuilding and connecting lines can be found in the companion album, *Paddington to Ealing*.

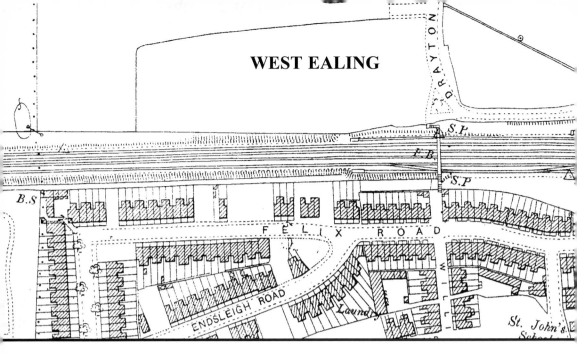

WEST EALING

V.   The 1895 map carried the name used from the opening of the station on 1st March 1871 until 1st July 1899. Note that although the old goods yard was on the south side, there were two sidings on the north side.

13.   A standard gauge down train stands on the mixed gauge main line and is viewed from the steps of the footbridge shown on the left of the map above. All the other lines in the picture were laid as standard gauge. (J.C.Gillham coll.)

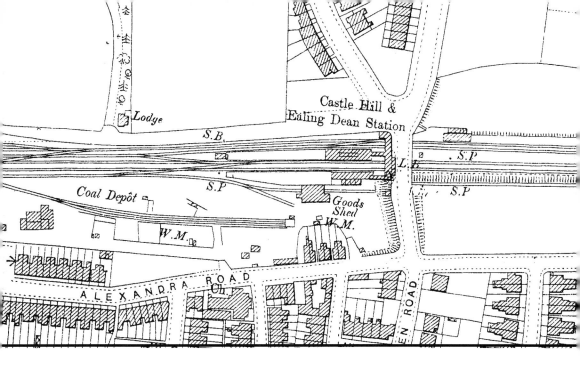

14.   A closer view of the station includes a ventilated van in the goods shed and the up local platform beyond the bridge. It would have been practical to site this platform opposite the others, but it seems that siding expansion had already been planned. (NRM)

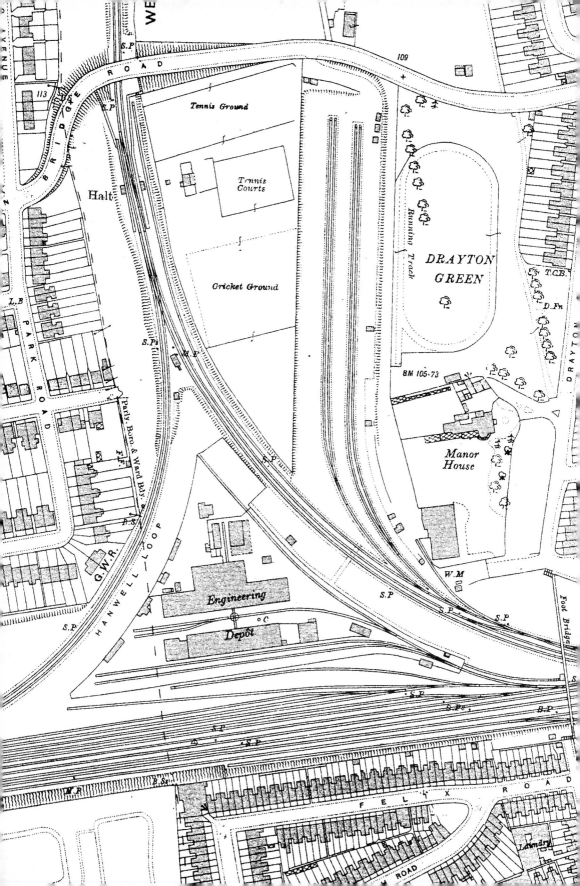

WE
109
113

BRIDGE ROAD

S.P.

Tennis Ground

Halt

Tennis Courts

Running Track

DRAYTON GREEN

T.C.B.

D.Fn

L.B

Cricket Ground

S.P.

M.P.

PARK ROAD

AVENUE

DRAYTON

BM 105·73

S.P.

Parly. Boro. & Ward Bdy.

Manor House

B.S.

G.W.R.

HANWELL LOOP

W.M

Engineering

W.M

S.P.

S.P.

S.P.

Foot Bridge

Depot

C

S.P.

S.P.

S.P.s

B.P.

S.P.

W.R.

B.S.

S.P.

FELIX ROAD

ROAD

Laundry

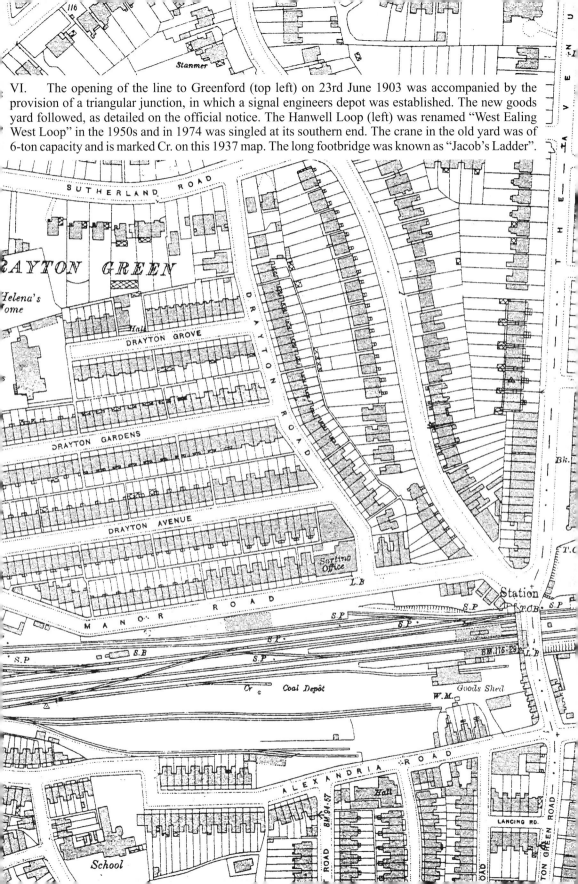

VI.   The opening of the line to Greenford (top left) on 23rd June 1903 was accompanied by the provision of a triangular junction, in which a signal engineers depot was established. The new goods yard followed, as detailed on the official notice. The Hanwell Loop (left) was renamed "West Ealing West Loop" in the 1950s and in 1974 was singled at its southern end. The crane in the old yard was of 6-ton capacity and is marked Cr. on this 1937 map. The long footbridge was known as "Jacob's Ladder".

GREAT WESTERN RAILWAY.

On 3rd February, 1908,

A NEW

Goods and Coal Depot

WILL BE OPENED AT

WEST EALING

(Entrances in Manor Road and Drayton Bridge Road),

FOR

Coal, Coke, Timber Bricks, Stone, Hay, Straw, and other descriptions of Mineral and Merchandise Traffic carried at rates which do not include collection or delivery

The New Depot will be convenient for Traders and others in the Districts of Ealing, West Ealing, and Hanwell.

There is extensive Siding and other accommodation in direct connection with the Company's Main Line, ensuring quick transit to and from all parts of the United Kingdom.

Information respecting rates and other arrangements can be obtained on application to Mr. W. E. DAVIES, West Ealing Goods Station ; to Mr. J. C. KINGETT, District Goods Manager, 23, Newgate Street, E.C. ; or to Mr. T. H. RENDELL, Chief Goods Manager, Paddington Station.

PADDINGTON STATION,   **JAMES C. INGLIS,**
   January, 1908.   *General Manager.*

2,000.   WYMAN & SONS, LTD., Printers, Fetter Lane, London, E.C., and Reading.—1018a.

15.   The isolated up local platform was numbered 4 and is seen from Drayton Green Road bridge. The early morning crowds were known as "daily breaders", until the importation of the term "commuter" from the USA. (Lens of Sutton)

16.   The footbridge provided a fine grandstand for this and several of the photographs that follow. No. 4917 *Crosswood Hall* heads empty milk tankers on 11th April 1955. They are bound for Whitland and are passing the signal box, which had a new 71-lever frame fitted on 20th March of that year. (R.C.Riley)

17.   No. 4700 heads the 12.05 Paddington to Plymouth on
10th August 1957 and has caught up with an earlier down local
train. 81A indicates that it was shedded at Old Oak Common.
(R.C.Riley)

18.   Three photographs from 14th August 1959 convey the atmosphere of the station at that time. Platforms 1 and 2 were hardly ever used by passengers, as expresses normally raced through. One such is headed by no. 5979 *Cruckton Hall*, obscured by shadow. Note the coupled chimneys on the booking hall. (J.C.Gillham)

19.   Passengers from the booking hall to platform 4 had to use the footbridge over the relief lines and then three flights of steps - north, west and east. The points are for the milk dock which was in use until about 1978. (J.C.Gillham)

20.	A westward panorama includes the old yard loading gauge, Jacob's Ladder footbridge, the signal box, which closed on 18th March 1968, and the milk dock, which began receiving bulk tankers in 1927. (J.C.Gillham)

21.	No. 6998 *Burton Agnes Hall* catches the afternoon sun as it passes over the junction points on 1st December 1962 with an up freight. Built in 1949, this locomotive is now usually to be found at the Didcot Railway Centre. A siding on the right served Pressings & Stampings Ltd until about 1966. (T.Wright)

22.	No. 50007 speeds east with the 09.45 from Weston-super-Mare on 20th September 1974, as class 35 no. D7018 waits to leave the yard with an engineers train. The former GWR premises behind it were acquired by Plasser & Theurer Ltd in 1969 and used for assembling their Austrian-built track maintenance equipment. Manufacture commenced here in 1977. (G.Gillham)

23.   Nos. 31110 and 31105 take the Greenford curve on 9th June 1978, with a train of oil tankers. Two ground frames were provided for the milk sidings and one for the Plasser (GB) Ltd. siding, lower right. (T.Heavyside)

24.   Plasser's 1984 building and security fence are evident as a "mixed" train runs towards Paddington on a gloomy day in March 1987. To the right of the train are three up loops and an engineers siding. (P.G.Barnes)

25.   The 08.51 from Paddington to Reading was recorded crossing from relief to main lines on 11th March 1989. Platform 1 had been removed in November 1973 and the old goods yard tracks were lifted in November 1968. (P.G.Barnes)

26.   Seen on the same day is no. 47602 departing with one of Plasser's products, while an up HST runs through platform 2 and under the new building that had been erected in 1987. (P.G.Barnes)

——————▶

27.   No. D1007 was derailed east of the station on 19th December 1973, due indirectly to a battery box lid falling from it. The scene witnessed here is the consequence of vandals derailing no. 50025 on 6th August 1989, while travelling from Oxford at 70mph. Seven people were injured. (J.C.Gillham)

——————▶

28.   No. 60025 *Joseph Lister* heads an oil train on 27th October 1993 and is about to pass under the footbridge. The term "Jacob's Ladder" is also applied to one close to Portsmouth & Southsea station. The Plasser Works has gates across three sidings on the right and two in the centre. (M. Turvey)

29.   A new booking office opened on 2nd May 1987 and new steps to the up local platform (still numbered 4) were provided (see pictures 25 and 26). A new platform, west of the bridge, was completed in 1991. This photograph is from 9th October 1999. (V.Mitchell)

30.   A class 165 Thames Turbo DMU, a type introduced in 1992, stands at the resurfaced platform 3 on 17th July 1996. Platform 2 had been fenced off and the new platform 4 has a temporary electrification mast near its edge. The track realignment allowed the relief lines to have the speed limit raised from 40 to 70mph. (J.C.Gillham)

HANWELL

VII.   The 1895 survey shows the semi-rural nature of the district and the relationship of the station to the town centre. This received electric trams along the High Street in 1901 (see *Shepherds Bush to Uxbridge Tramways* - Middleton Press). They competed with the GWR as far as Southall.

31.	A local train approaches on the up relief line and nears the sign bearing the words AND ELTHORNE. This suffix was in use from 1st April 1896 to 5th May 1974. The station opened on 1st December 1838 and was completely rebuilt in 1877. (Lens of Sutton)

32.	A westward view from 1919 features the original route, the wide space between the tracks being a legacy from the broad gauge era. The wide island platform resulted in curves on the new lines, seen more clearly in the previous picture. (NRM)

33.   No. 3688 plods along the up relief line in November 1959 with very assorted goods wagons, probably bound for Acton, where much marshalling was undertaken. The locomotive was one of the large class of 5700 0-6-0PTs introduced in 1929. (T.Wright)

34.   Heading a milk train on the down relief line is no. 5060 *Earl of Berkeley*, one of the successful "Castle" class 4-6-0s. The 45-lever signal box had been just beyond the right border of the picture until 20th March 1955. There was also a Hanwell West box until 1934. (Lens of Sutton)

35. The imposing south elevation faced the town and was photographed in May 1961. Passengers had to be in good physical condition to climb the many stairs to the platform level. This building was demolished in 1977 and the entrance bricked up. (J.C.Gillham)

⟶

36. The north elevation was recorded at the same time. There was generous accommodation for both staff and passengers. Aesthetic considerations were made during electrification in the mid-1990s and circular masts were erected here. The ticket office is now on the ground floor. (J.C.Gillham)

6049 3rd ■ SINGLE   SINGLE ■ 3rd 6049
West Ealing to
West Ealing   West Ealing
8.16   8.16
Hanwell&Elthorne   Hanwell&Elthorne
HANWELL & ELTHORNE
(W)   2d   FARE   2d   (W)
ForConditions see over ForConditions see over

⟶

37. Seen in 1991 is the result of a restoration programme, which included the cleaning of the fine polychromatic brickwork, the fitting of electrified gas lanterns and the refurbishment of an old sign. Platform 1, on the down main line, had been removed. (P.G.Barnes)

WHARNCLIFFE VIADUCT

38.   The Brent Valley is crossed west of Hanwell on this fine 297 yd long 65ft high eight-span viaduct, work on which began in February 1836. Spotters are in action in July 1958. The 55-yd long Hanwell Viaduct is insignificant in comparison and is immediately east of this one. (A.E.Bennett)

39.   The structure was named after Lord Wharncliffe, who was noted for having headed the inquiry into the wisdom of constructing Box Tunnel, further west on the route to Bristol. The tranquil River Brent and an ubiquitous Pannier tank are seen in this northward view from 1961. (J.C.Gillham)

EAST OF SOUTHALL

40.   The first engine shed on this site opened in 1859 and had a single road, plus a 45ft turntable. The shed illustrated was erected in 1884 to house 18 locomotives and was provided with a 65ft turntable in 1909. The repair shop is on the left. (LPC/NRM)

(lower left)
41. The engine shed is on the right as we witness no. 4960 *Pyle Hall* passing the extended goods shed on 10th August 1957. The train is the 2.35pm Paddington to Weston-super-Mare via Devizes. Obscured by the signal gantry is the 48-lever East Junction box, which closed on 13th May 1968. (R.C.Riley)

(below)
42. The engine shed was rebuilt and enlarged in 1954, but it had no doors and the repair shop was further east. From left to right on 20th July 1958 are nos. 1446, 6148, W21W, 3812, 90188, 6125 and 2890. The railcar's seats became filthy in this environment. (A.E.Bennett)

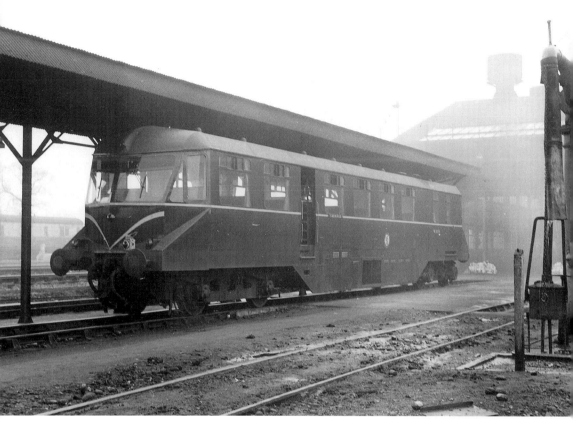

43.   Standing outside the shed on 3rd April 1960 was green-liveried railcar no. W32W. Like others in the GWR fleet, its engine and transmission had been made by AEC at their works, which was situated immediately south of this depot. (T.Wright)

44.   Exhaust obscures many of the nearly redundant cattle wagons and much of East Yard on 28th April 1963, as no. 6018 *King Henry VI* works a Stephenson Locomotive Society special train. It was billed as the last working of a "King". Steam ceased at this shed on 31st December 1965. (R.C.Riley)

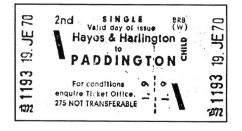

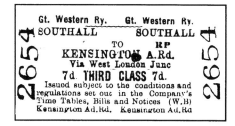

45.   The shed was adapted for the stabling of DMUs, a purpose which it served until November 1986. A coal train from Acton Yard to the Brentford branch moves over the crossovers on 21st March 1974, headed by class 35 no. D7028. It will have to reverse at one of the sidings west of the station. (G.Gillham)

46.   The north side of the goods shed and part of East Yard were recorded in 1973. Goods traffic ceased here in March 1965, but Shell Mex & BP opened some fuel sidings in the distance, in 1967. (J.C.Gillham)

47.   The GWR Preservation Group moved its collection from the goods shed to the former engine shed in 1988 and opened it to the public in 1994. One of the resident locomotives was 4-6-2 no. 35028 *Clan Line*, which is close to the water tower as no. 56043 passes with Purley-Merehead empty stone wagons on 22nd June 1991. (P.G.Barnes)

48.	Access to the GWRPG's collection was at weekends via the public footbridge and the steps on the left. The water softener and coal stage had long gone, but the tank was a useful relic. No. 59102 is hauling the 10.00 Allington to Whatley Quarry empties over the crossover on 22nd June 1991. (P.G.Barnes)

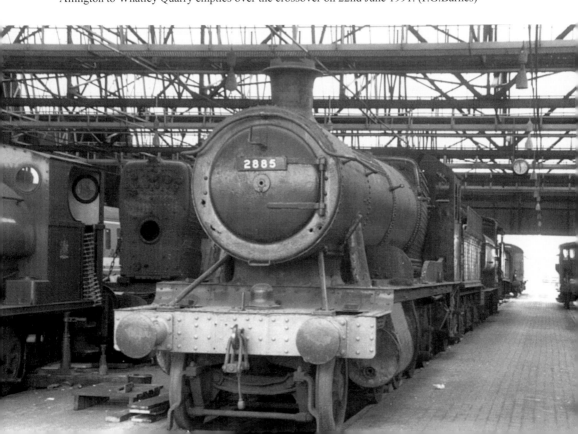

49. The 10.32 Swansea to Paddington HST, travelling at nearly 100mph, struck the middle of an empty stone train, which was crossing from the down relief to the down main line at 13.20 on 19th September 1997. The HST driver had apparently failed to observe adverse signals and his automatic train protection equipment was faulty. Seven died. (K.Brunt)

←————————

50. Known as the "Southall Railway Centre", the shed housed ex-GWR 2-8-0 no. 2885, 2-6-2T no. 4110, 0-6-0PT no. 9682 (built by BR in 1949) and ex-LNER class J94 no. 68078, together with two DMUs, several industrial locomotives and much other stock. The date is 15th May 1996. (M.Turvey)

————————→

51. The sheds became the base for ex-LNER no. 4472 Flying Scotsman, seen here at the repair shop on 4th September 1999. The GWRPG lease had been terminated in July 1997 in favour of Flying Scotsman Railways, but much of the Group's stock was still on site two years later. (K.Brunt)

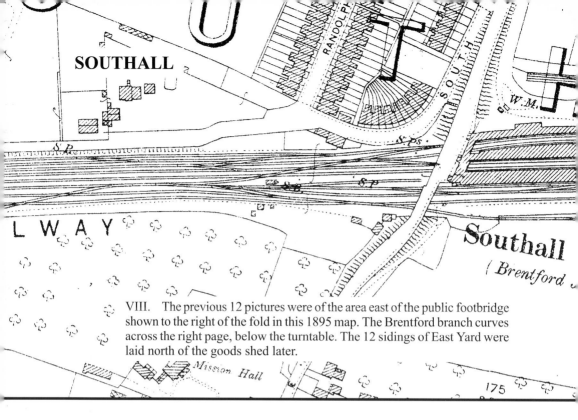

SOUTHALL

LWAY

Southall

(Brentford J

VIII.   The previous 12 pictures were of the area east of the public footbridge shown to the right of the fold in this 1895 map. The Brentford branch curves across the right page, below the turntable. The 12 sidings of East Yard were laid north of the goods shed later.

Mission Hall

175

52.   The up side building and goods shed were drawn in the broad gauge era, probably in about 1850. Major alterations were carried out prior to the quadrupling, which took place east hereof in 1877 and westwards in 1879. (British Rail)

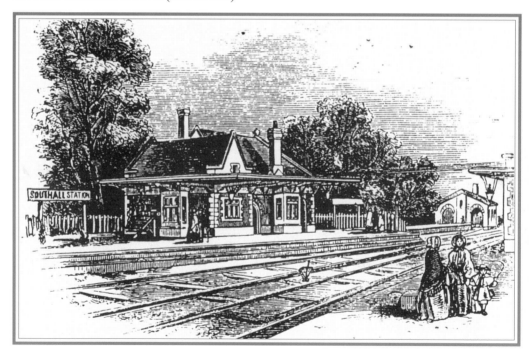

SOUTHALL STATION

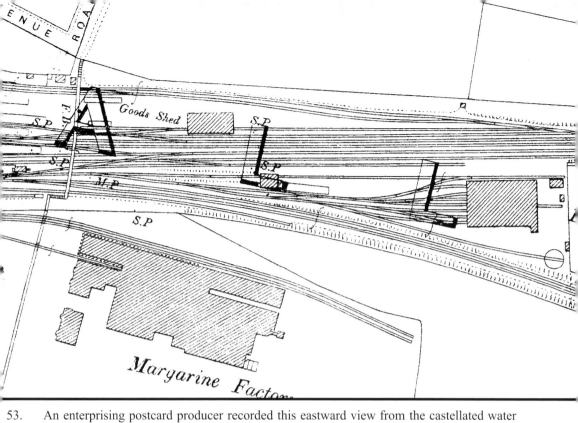

Goods Shed

S.P

S.P

S.P

S.P

M.P

S.P

S.P

Margarine Factory

53.   An enterprising postcard producer recorded this eastward view from the castellated water tower that features in subsequent pictures. In the distance are the goods shed, the engine shed and the margarine factory, but the platforms are obscured by the 1877 building. (Lens of Sutton)

54. The main lines are on the left of centre, the relief lines in the centre and the bay platform is on the right. Note that the through train is formed of clerestory-roofed coaches, but the local train has shorter vehicles. Sadly the photographer missed the buffers. (Lens of Sutton)

55. The line at the far left platform in this 1919 view ended at buffers near the bridge and was used by Brentford branch trains. The bay line and the parallel loop line ended on a turntable. Colour light signalling was introduced between here and Paddington in 1933. (LGRP/NRM)

56. "Castle" class no. 5055 *Earl of Eldon* speeds towards Paddington on 10th August 1957, while passengers wait for an up local train. On the left is the 123-lever Southall East Station box, which was in use until 13th May 1968. (R.C.Riley)

57.   In the background are the tower of the 1905 water softener and the public footbridge, from which many of the photographs were taken. No. 4673 is standing on the "Down Through Line". To the left of it is "Up Through" and on the right is "Branch Reversible". The date and the photographer are not known. (J.C.Gillham coll.)

——————————▶

58.   The characteristic GWR tapered towers surmounted by cast iron tracery and the gracious canopies survived Adolf Hitler's activities and could still be enjoyed in the 1960s. So could parking your Morris or Ford in front of the station. (Lens of Sutton)

——————————▶

59.   The public footbridge traverses this 1974 photograph of the north side of the station; a turntable had once been situated in the foreground and a cattle pen had stood on the dock on the extreme left. The bay was used for mail traffic. The goods yard had closed on 2nd January 1967. (J.C.Gillham)

60.   By 1974, BR's maintenance cost-cutting measures had included pruning the towers and lopping off the northern wing. There were few traditionalists remaining locally to be concerned by then, the area having become home to immigrants from Southern Asia. (J.C.Gillham)

61.   As no. 46023 passes through with an up stone train on 9th June 1978, we can see the glazed footway that replaced the northern wing and also note that the canopy on the island platform had been reduced in length. There were no significant alterations here in the subsequent 22 years, apart from the provision of bilingual station nameboards, showing Punjabi, in 1998. (T.Heavyside)

WEST OF SOUTHALL

62.   A westward panorama from the road bridge in 1974 features West Yard, which comprised
(from south to north) Up Yard (three sidings), Down Yard (six sidings) Down Goods and No. 2 Up
Goods. (No. 1 was north of the relief lines). There had been sidings on the left for Bachelors Peas
and Le Grand Sutcliffe. The brickwork on the right was associated with the 100-lever West Station
box, which functioned until 13th May 1968. (J.C.Gillham)

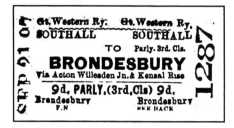

63.   Closed on the same day was West Junction box, which had 55 levers and was situated at the far end of the yard. Beyond it there had been sidings for Crown Cork, British Thomson Houston, International Tea Company, Scotts Emulsion and a wallpaper factory. Seen on 27th September 1981 is an empty refuse train reversing into the yard, prior to traversing the remaining part of the Brentford branch. Such reversals have not been necessary since track alterations were made in March 1995.
(T.Heavyside)

IX.   The gasworks siding was an extension of one of Southall's two carriage sidings when this 1895 edition was issued. The works later had two additional sidings, both branching from the Up Goods line. "Path" refers to the Grand Junction Canal towpath. A small private works was built in 1865 and acquired by the Brentford Gas Company. The works shown was opened in 1869. It obtained most of its coal by canal, but by the 1950s the majority came by rail - about 160,000 tons per annum. It ceased to use coal in 1965, oil arriving by barge and later by pipeline. By-products and chemical traffic was conveyed by rail until 1961. Most of the coal in the 1930s was brought in block trains from the GWR's Brentford Docks, 50 wagons having been built specially for the traffic.

64.   Manning Wardle 0-4-0ST no. 2 of 1874 is on one of the high level sidings, while a horse enjoys its nosebag. No. 1 was an 0-6-0ST from the same builder and worked the low level sidings. Both were scrapped at about the time that the Gas, Light & Coke Company took over in 1926. Of the five subsequent locomotives, three have been preserved. That number had been in use simultaneously in the 1950s. (British Gas)

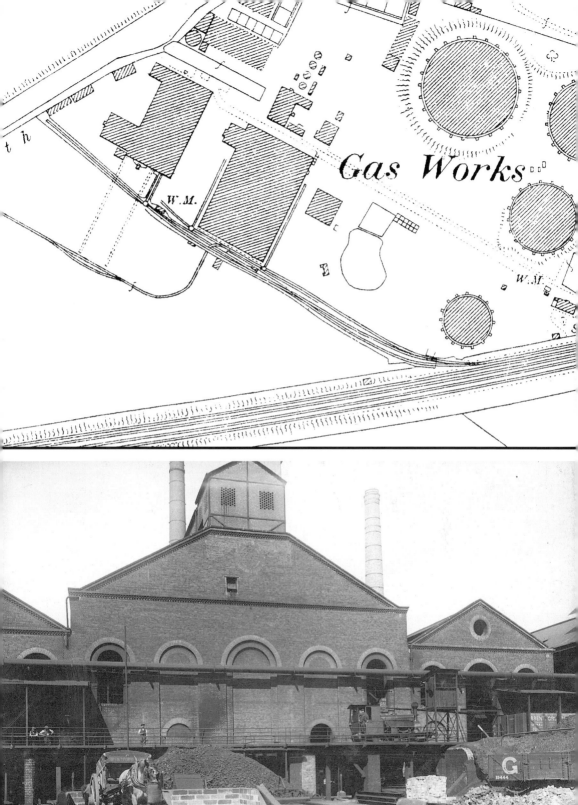

Gas Works

X.   The maximum consumption of coal was an amazing 700 tons per day after the plant had been doubled in size after World War II. It was nationalised and came under the North Thames Gas Board in 1949. By 1954 most of the coal was coming

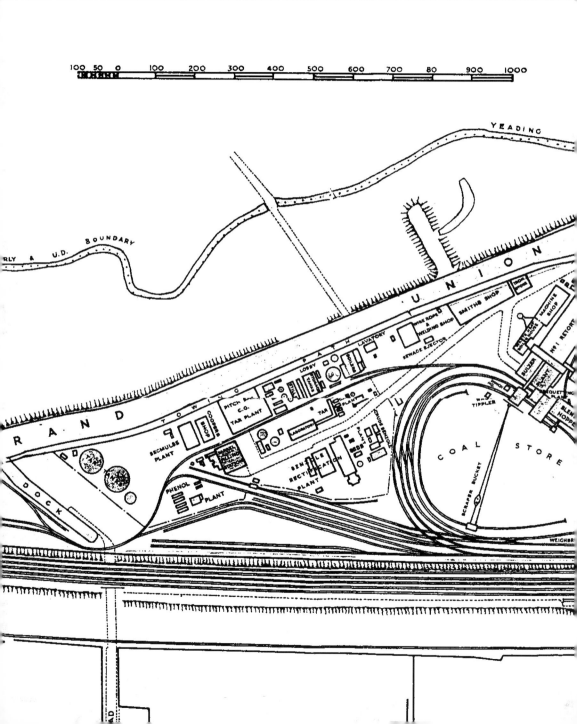

by rail direct from Derbyshire and Yorkshire. Vast amounts of coke were despatched by rail, also tar and benzole until 1961. This plan dates from about 1940, but the GWR sidings (lower right) are not shown fully.

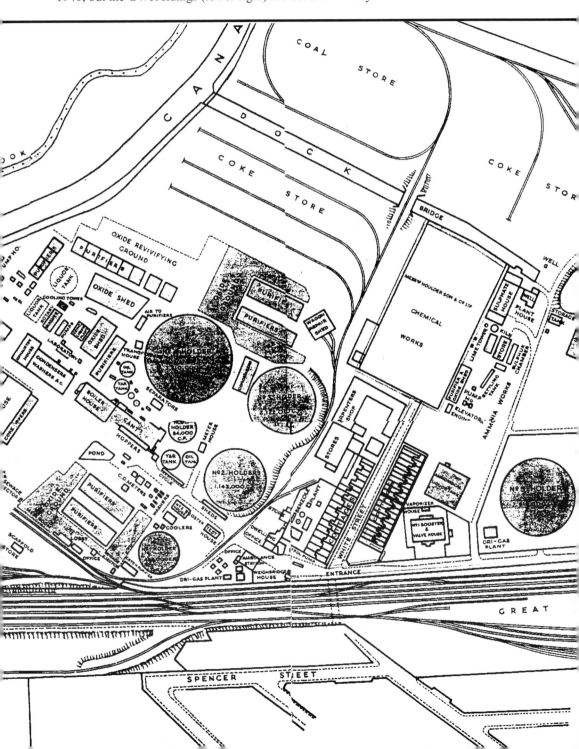

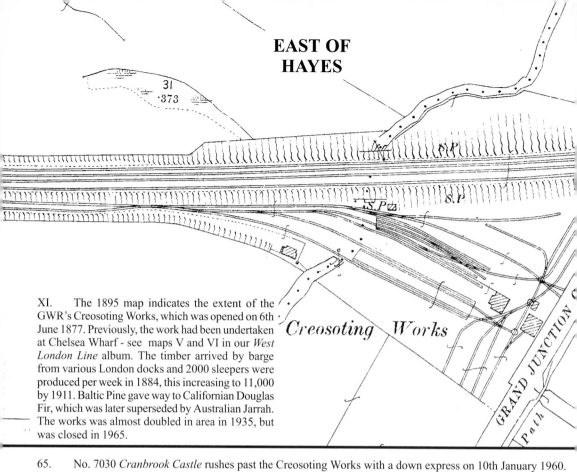

31
·373

S.P

S.P

Creosoting Works

GRAND JUNCTION C

Path

XI.   The 1895 map indicates the extent of the GWR's Creosoting Works, which was opened on 6th June 1877. Previously, the work had been undertaken at Chelsea Wharf - see maps V and VI in our *West London Line* album. The timber arrived by barge from various London docks and 2000 sleepers were produced per week in 1884, this increasing to 11,000 by 1911. Baltic Pine gave way to Californian Douglas Fir, which was later superseded by Australian Jarrah. The works was almost doubled in area in 1935, but was closed in 1965.

65.   No. 7030 *Cranbrook Castle* rushes past the Creosoting Works with a down express on 10th January 1960. The creosoting took place in giant autoclaves in which up to 350 sleepers were placed on trolleys. The vessels were first evacuated and then filled with the fluid, which was a gas works by-product, at 120 degrees F and pressurised at 200 lb/sq in for over one hour. (T.Wright)

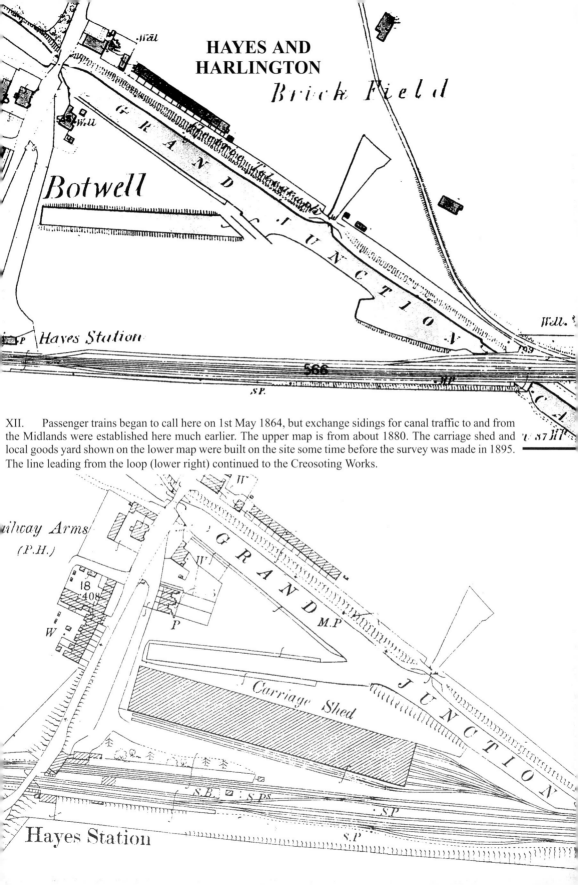

HAYES AND HARLINGTON

Brick Field

Botwell

GRAND JUNCTION

Haves Station

Wall.

Wall.

566

S.P.

XII.   Passenger trains began to call here on 1st May 1864, but exchange sidings for canal traffic to and from the Midlands were established here much earlier. The upper map is from about 1880. The carriage shed and local goods yard shown on the lower map were built on the site some time before the survey was made in 1895. The line leading from the loop (lower right) continued to the Creosoting Works.

ihcay Arms
(P.H.)

GRAND

M.P

JUNCTION

Carriage Shed

18
408

W

P

W

S.B.   SPs

S.P

Hayes Station

S.P

66.   The line to the Creosoting Works is near the signal in this eastward postcard view. A private siding was laid in the direction of the new factory for Nesfood. Another was put in parallel to the canal for the British Electric Transformer Company. (Lens of Sutton)

67.   A westward glance reveals that the second station buildings were constructed on the bridge over the 1879 relief lines. The suffix AND HARLINGTON was added on 22nd November 1897. (Lens of Sutton)

68.   A 1919 panorama includes the wide footbridge which had probably been added to cope with the traffic generated by the rapid industrialisation of the area. Beyond the bridge, sidings were provided for The Gramophone Company, later known as EMI. (LGRP/NRM)

69.   A photograph from August 1958 shows the full extent of the footbridge and the three sidings of the down yard. The box had an 80-lever frame from 1928 until closure on 10th June 1968. No fewer than eight firms had the use of private sidings in 1938. (R.C.Riley)

70.   No. 5957 *Hutton Hall* is on the left with the 12.25 Paddington to Reading on 20th June 1959 and alongside is 2-6-2T no. 6117 with the 12.36 Paddington to Windsor. The extensive goods yards were closed on 2nd January 1967; a 10-ton crane had once been available. (H.C.Casserley)

71.   Looking west on 12th May 1990, we witness the passage of no. 50031 with the 11.18 York to Paddington. On the right is the Dawley goods loop, which had been added in November 1942. The vacant space had been occupied by two carriage sidings from about 1925 to 1968. The 24-lever Dawley box had been on the left in the distance until closure on 7th January 1963. Bourne Bridge carries Dawley Road. (P.G.Barnes)

72.   Tarmac Roadstone established a new plant north-east of the station in 1968, the stone arriving in 1125 tonne batches from Markfield in Leicestershire. No. 56044 was recorded with ARC wagons from Whatley in Somerset on 12th May 1990. (P.G.Barnes)

73.   Thames Turbos of this type have provided the local service since 1992; this example was photographed working the 14.52 from Reading on 17th September 1995. All four platforms were still usable, but there was no building on the seldom used no. 1. The bay on the right was soon to receive overhead electrification. (M.J.Stretton)

74.   The electrification train, seen on 17th September 1995, was fitted with extendable drills, an excavator, cement hoppers and other stores and equipment. The first mast was erected in December 1994 and the last in February 1997. A separate train was used for wiring. (M.J.Stretton)

75.   The station was rebuilt in 1962, the previous building having been neglected for many years. This is a 1996 view; the east elevation is included in picture 73. (J.C.Gillham)

HEATHROW JUNCTION

76.   Work on a flyover for up trains from Heathrow began in September 1993, the first task being the slewing northwards of both relief lines to create a space between. This is the state of progress on 7th October 1996, long before masts and wires cluttered the skyline. (J.C.Gillham)

77.   A temporary station (left) was opened on 19th January 1998, while the terminus was being completed. The tracks to the latter have a scissors crossover (centre) at the approach to the mouth of the four-mile long tunnel. A gauging train hauled by diesel no. 47976 tested the route on 19th November 1997, soon after this photo had been taken. (A.Spencer)

78.   No. 332005 was recorded at Heathrow Junction on 12th January 1998 on a test run. Three-coach formations were used to this short-lived station, with four being the norm until September, since when the units have been coupled in pairs. The fleet is composed of 14 four-car units. (A.Spencer)

79.   A fleet of Plaxton-bodied DAF buses was provided to complete the link to the Airport. FastTrain was the marketing name employed. The station and the buses were used for only four months. (B.Morrison)

HEATHROW AIRPORT

80.   The branch ends at Terminal 4, about 30 metres below the surface. It came into use on 25th May 1998. An intermediate station was opened on the same day at Heathrow Central, this serving Terminals 1-3. It was here that the atrium above the station collapsed on 21st October 1994, during its construction. A fine of £1.2m followed. The track is single between the two airport stations. The single fare to Paddington, initially £5, was increased to £10 after four weeks and to £15 at peak times in June 1999, after a £2m operating loss had been announced. (B.Morrison)

WEST DRAYTON

81.   Being slow moving, freight was usually conveyed on the relief lines. The leading wagons are marked GW and so the large lumps of coal are probably destined for locomotive fireboxes. The goods shed is in the background and the locomotive is "Duke" class 4-4-0 no. 3261 *Saint Germans*. (Lens of Sutton)

82.   A fine eastward view from 1919 includes the usual rash of enamelled metal advertisements, plus a weighing machine for curious passengers and a water column for locomotives on the down relief line. (LGRP/NRM)

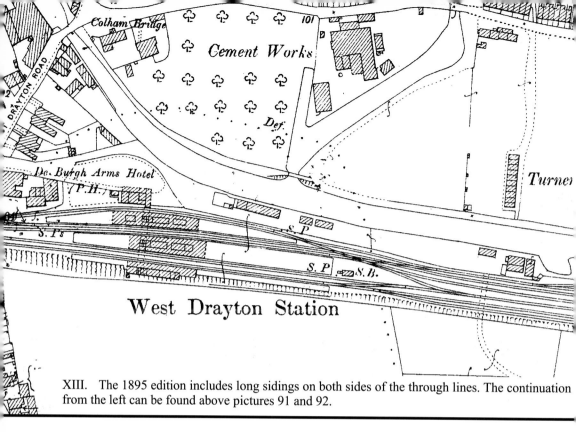

West Drayton Station

XIII. The 1895 edition includes long sidings on both sides of the through lines. The continuation from the left can be found above pictures 91 and 92.

83.   The long down refuge siding disappears into the mist as no. 6018 *King Henry VI* runs through with "The Merchant Venturer" on 30th June 1951. This was the 11.15am Paddington to Weston-super-Mare. The siding had earlier served Admiralty Aircraft Construction and the Power Plant Company. East Box was in use from 25th May 1936 to 9th February 1964; it had 69 levers. (N.W.Sprinks)

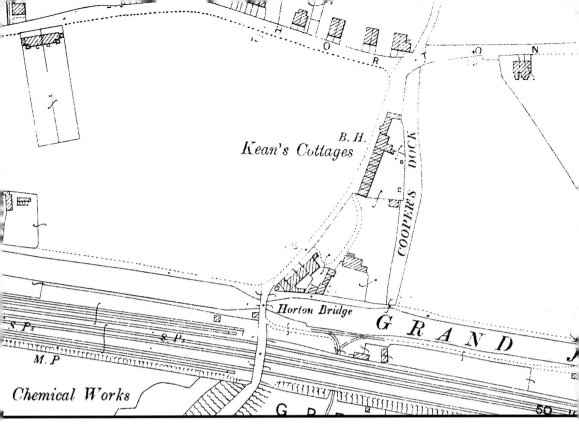

84.   Not seen before in this volume is the "Britannia" class, a type introduced in 1951. No. 70027 *Rising Star* coasts past platform 1 on 27th April 1960, with the "Red Dragon", the 5.55pm Paddington to Carmarthen. (T.Wright)

85.   Eastbound past the perforated backing signals on 21st May 1960 is 2800 class 2-8-0 no. 2862 with freight from Severn Tunnel Junction. On the left is the 90-lever West Box, which was in use until 16th May 1960, when it was replaced by the one seen in picture 91. (T.Wright)

86.   Two photos taken from platform 1 in about 1960 include the goods yard in the background. This shows the full name used from 1895 to 1974. Branch services for passengers ceased to Uxbridge on 10th September 1962 and to Staines on 29th March 1965. (Lens of Sutton)

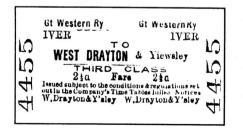

87.   Trains to both branches departed from platform 5 at which a shunting operation can be seen in this view. Services were operated by ex-GWR railcars or autotrains. (Lens of Sutton)

88. Looking west from platform 2 on 12th May 1990, we see the up goods line from Iver on the right. Curving from it is the goods line to Colnbrook (the limit of operation on the Staines branch) and the West Drayton Coal Concentration Depot. No. 50036 *Victorious* is working the 12.00 from Oxford. (P.G.Barnes)

89. The entrance is on the north side of the railway and was photographed in 1999, although it had changed little since the previous century. It had come into use on 9th August 1884. The previous station had been on the other side of the road; this had opened on 4th June 1838. (V.Mitchell)

90. A Thames Turbo has just passed the coal sidings on 14th September 1996. The area was redeveloped in 1963 to create a mechanised depot capable of distributing 200,000 tons per annum, with peaks of 1200 tons per day. Coal ceased to be received by rail on 7th April 1999. The bridge over which the train is travelling was rebuilt in 1960. (P.G.Barnes)

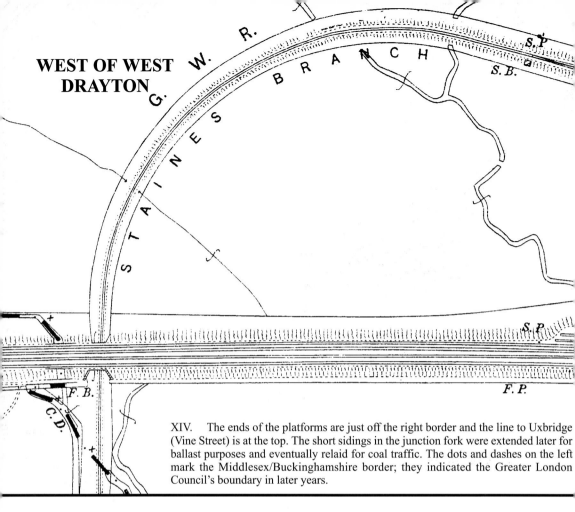

WEST OF WEST DRAYTON

G. W. R.

STAINES BRANCH

S.P.
S.B.

S.P.

F.B.

C.D.

F.P.

XIV.   The ends of the platforms are just off the right border and the line to Uxbridge (Vine Street) is at the top. The short sidings in the junction fork were extended later for ballast purposes and eventually relaid for coal traffic. The dots and dashes on the left mark the Middlesex/Buckinghamshire border; they indicated the Greater London Council's boundary in later years.

91.   The junction of the Uxbridge and Staines lines is in the foreground of this 1965 photograph. In the background is the 66-lever signal box, which was used from 16th May 1960 until 21st September 1970. (J.C.Gillham)

WHISTLE

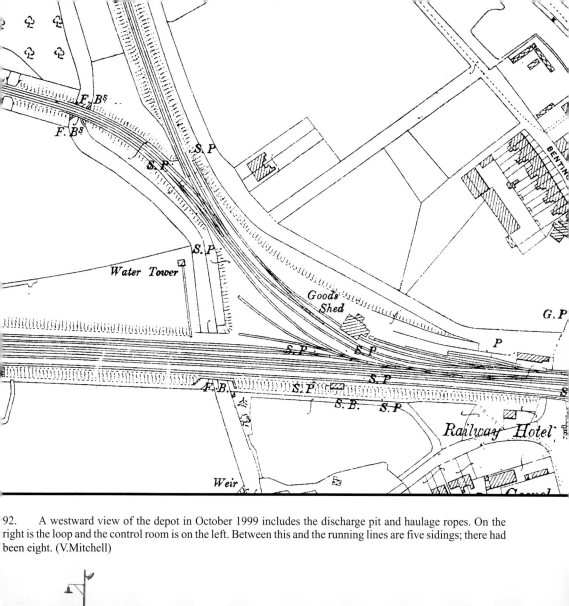

Water Tower

Goods
Shed

Weir

Railway Hotel

92.   A westward view of the depot in October 1999 includes the discharge pit and haulage ropes. On the right is the loop and the control room is on the left. Between this and the running lines are five sidings; there had been eight. (V.Mitchell)

IVER

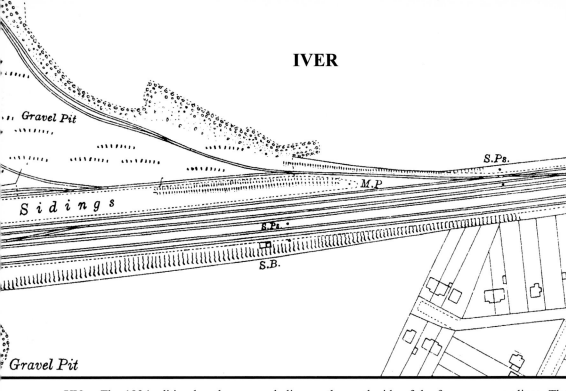

XV.   The 1934 edition has the up goods line on the north side of the four passenger lines. The gravel pits were worked by Road & Rail Aggregates and F.Wells. On the left is Iver signal box, which functioned until 14th October 1963 and had 34 levers.

93.   The station opened much later than the others, on 1st December 1924, as part of a scheme for extensive residential development. Note that the down main platform was devoid of a canopy, as few trains stopped at it. The ringed signal on the left was for the goods line. (Lens of Sutton)

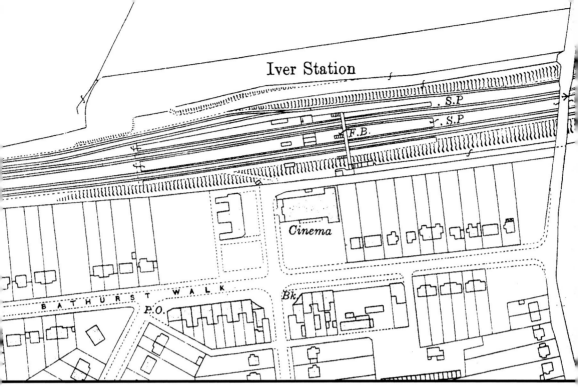

94.   On the right is the up goods line, which was opened on 22nd March 1914, between Iver and West Drayton. The small station buildings are dwarfed by the massive cinema, an essential part of life in the pre-TV era. Iver handled only wagon-loads of coal or minerals. (Lens of Sutton)

95.   The unimpressive main entrance is on the left, but it was not visible from the shopping area. The ticket office projected from the back, as can be seen from the previous photograph. This is a 1959 view. (H.C.Casserley)

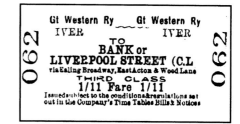

96.   After an oil train fire at Langley, many of the wagons were shunted into the coal sidings out of public view, but they were photographed in October 1973 with *DANGER* chalked on their buffers. All goods traffic had ceased on 2nd January 1964; this had included domestic coal for local merchants. The sidings remained in place until about 1989. (T.Wright)

97.   One of the "Blue Pullmans" was photographed on the down main line in 1973, with some of Iver's many "semis" in the background. There were two such trains to Swansea and one to Bristol every weekday at that time, each passenger paying a £1 supplement. They were in use from 1960 until 1975. (T.Wright)

98. The "Western" class 52s were regular performers in the 1970s, regular use ending in 1977. This example is no. D1034 *Western Dragon* and is seen on the up main line on 6th August 1974, with a train of Mk.2 coaches. (G.Gillham)

99. Three passenger and one breakdown train were all to be seen on 17th September 1977. The latter was attending the derailment of no. 50033 in the siding that served Bison's concrete works. The goods line begins near the bridge in the distance. (T.Wright)

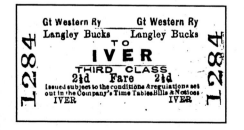

100. An up local train was photographed from the 1924 footbridge on 25th September 1999. The picture includes the up goods line and one of the two new waiting shelters. In place of glass (which was broken frequently) are tasteful iron screens in which is incorporated the logos of Thames Trains. (T.Wright)

LANGLEY

Langley Station
S.P.
P.
S.P.
F.P.
North Star
(P.H.)
S.P.
S.B.
F.P.
S.P.
S.P.
S.B.
S.

XVI.   The 1899 survey includes a long headshunt on the north side and a refuge siding on the south. The population grew from 2801 in 1901 to 6115 in 1951. The tramway ran from the brickworks to a canal wharf.

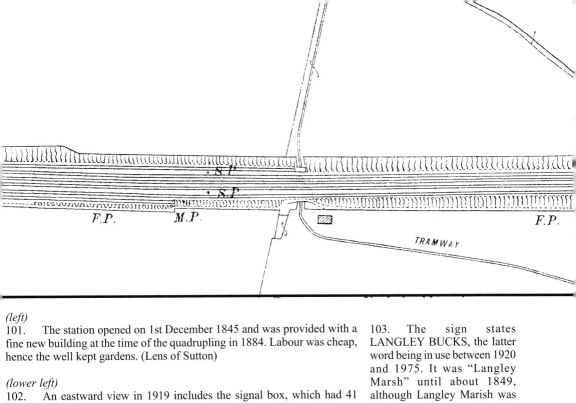

S.P

S.P

F.P.   *M.P.*   *F.P.*

TRAMWAY

(left)
101.   The station opened on 1st December 1845 and was provided with a fine new building at the time of the quadrupling in 1884. Labour was cheap, hence the well kept gardens. (Lens of Sutton)

(lower left)
102.   An eastward view in 1919 includes the signal box, which had 41 levers and closed on 14th October 1963, and the refuge siding, which was used for holding slow goods trains. This was taken out of use in November 1962. The poles remind us that the route had an electric telegraph from its opening in 1838. (LGRP/NRM)

103.   The sign states LANGLEY BUCKS, the latter word being in use between 1920 and 1975. It was "Langley Marsh" until about 1849, although Langley Marsh was the name of the parish. The footbridge roof had gone by 1960, but little else had changed otherwise. (Lens of Sutton)

104.   No. 6913 *Levens Hall* works up the relief line on 9th December 1962, with a van train. The single coach had probably been included in a down night train. Engine cleaning was uncommon by that time. (T.Wright)

105.   The 6-ton crane and the loading gauge are included in this view of track lifting commencing on 3rd May 1964; goods facilities were withdrawn on 6th January prior. The curved line had served B.R. & N.C.Stacey, suppliers of sawdust to the Staines Linoleum Works, which had its own sidings. The points are near the site of the buffers of the oil terminal that opened on 15th June 1969. (T.Wright)

106.   A train discharging 680 tons of petrol and 370 tons of diesel fuel in the oil terminal on 5th October 1973 moved, exploded and caught fire. Over 100 firemen took five hours to deal with the problem, while residents were moved away and trains were suspended. (T.Wright)

107.   Single unit no. L129 was working a shuttle service to and from Slough in March 1986, due to permanent way work. The route is fairly straight, but one of its curves is evident here. (T.Wright)

108. The north elevation was photographed in May 1986, shortly before a major renovation programme on the 102 year-old building commenced. Strong local opposition prevented demolition of the building. (T.Wright)

109. Work on the building was still in progress as an HST unusually used the down relief line on 11th December 1988. In the background are the three sidings and the storage tanks of the Total Oil Terminal. (T.Wright)

110. Nos. 37696 and 37697 failed to stop at the end of the up refuge siding and almost descended into Mansion Lane on 28th December 1989. The crossovers of Dolphin Junction are west of the station. (T.Wright)

EAST OF SLOUGH

XVII. The gasworks was established on this site in 1902 and is shown on the 1923 edition. It was expanded in 1935-41, during which time it became part of the South Eastern Gas Corporation. Coal consumed rose from 9500 tons in 1923 to 69,000 tons in 1945. A Falcon 0-4-0ST was purchased in 1937. Three other steam and three Hibberd diesels are known to have worked here. Batches of up to 20 coal wagons were routed through the siding of Naylor Bros.

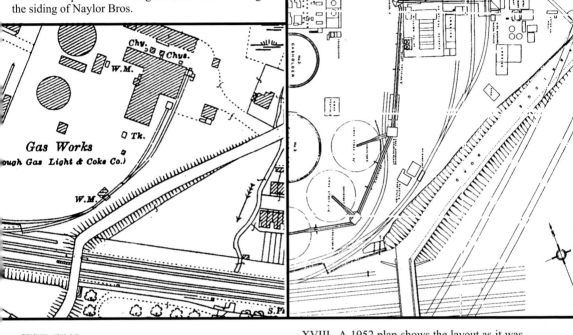

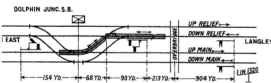

XVIII. A 1952 plan shows the layout as it was until cessation of coal gas production in March 1965. Rail traffic then ceased in favour of oil by pipeline. Coal was unloaded using a tippler on the east siding and coke was loaded from a conveyor over the west siding. The plant was altered several times over the years. A siding was added east of Dolphin Junction and north of the main lines for Starch Products Ltd in 1938.

XIX. Dolphin Junction gave connections between all four running lines east of the station and was controlled by a 47-lever box until 14th October 1973. Its signalman failed to ensure that a down goods train had stopped on 2nd July 1941, before allowing an up train from Plymouth to cross in front of it, at 2.55am. Five passengers were killed. (Railway Magazine)

111. The goods engine (right) was on loan from the LMS and was 2-8-0 no. 8293. The up passenger train was hauled by 4-6-0 no. 4091 *Dudley Castle*. Automatic Train Control was in use on the route, but the loaned engine was not fitted with the equipment.
(Railway Magazine)

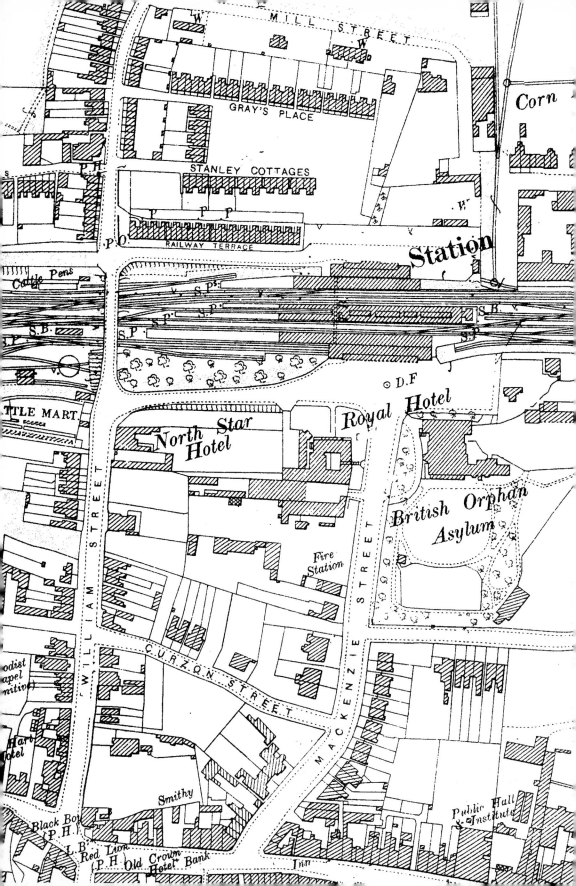

MILL STREET

W

W

Corn

GRAY'S PLACE

STANLEY COTTAGES

P P P

P.O.

RAILWAY TERRACE

Station

Cattle Pens

S.P.   S.P.

S.P.   S.P.

S.B.

S.B.

S.P.

V.

D.F

TLE MART

North Star
Hotel

Royal Hotel

British Orphan
Asylum

WILLIAM STREET

MACKENZIE STREET

Fire
Station

odist
apel
mitive)

CURZON STREET

Hart
Hotel

Smithy

Public Hall
& Institute

Black Boy
(P.H.)

L.B.

Red Lion
P.H

Old Crown
Hotel Bank

Inn

SLOUGH

XX.   The upper of the five lines on the right of this 1899 map was a headshunt for the siding to the Gotha Iron Works. The triangular junction for the 1849 Windsor Branch and the adjacent locomotive shed are beyond the left border. The gasworks shown on the right page closed in 1902.

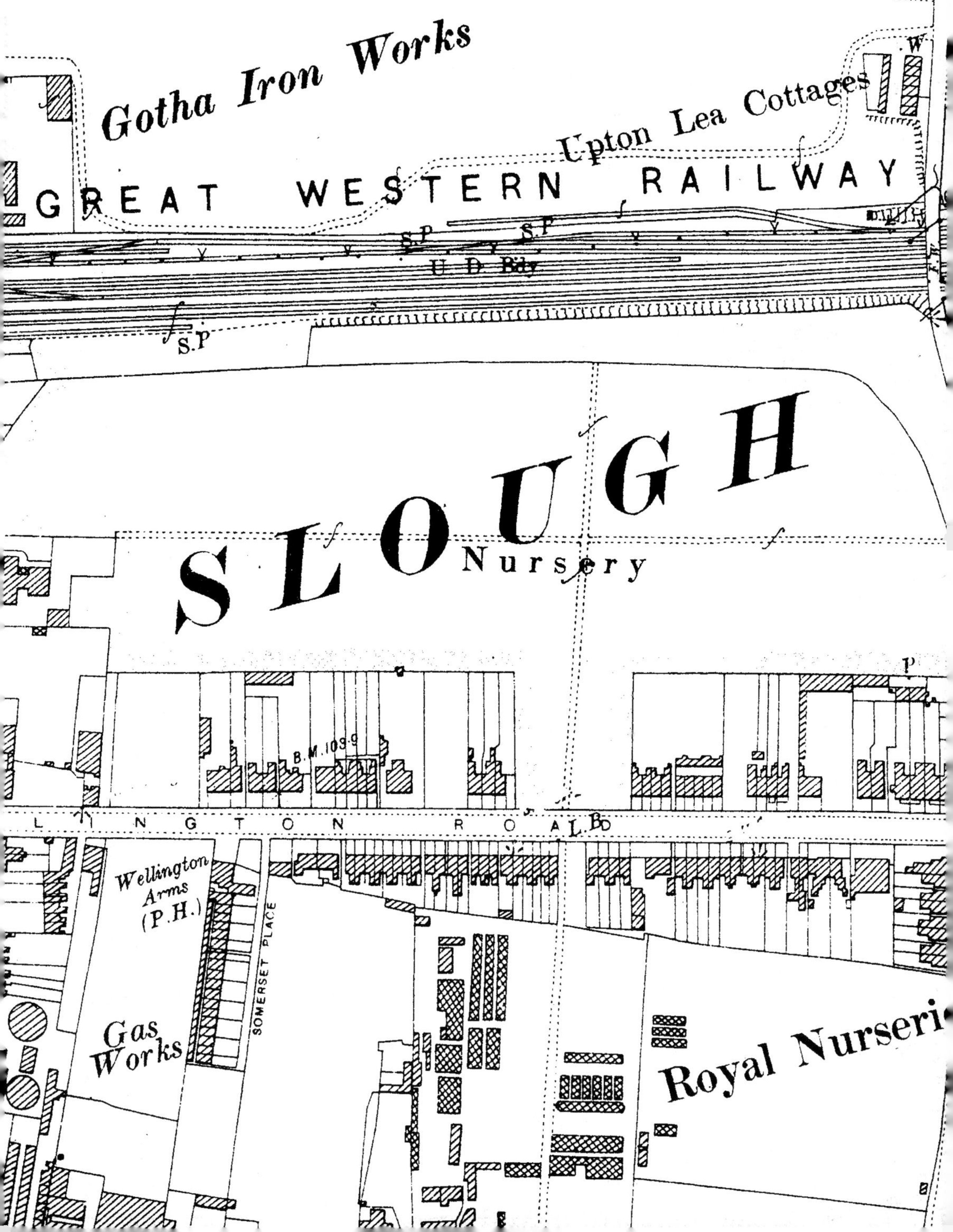

Gotha Iron Works

Upton Lea Cottages

GREAT WESTERN RAILWAY

S.P   S.P

U. D. Bdy

S.P

S.P

SLOUGH

Nursery

B.M.109·9

L I N G T O N   R O A L. Bd

Wellington
Arms
(P.H.)

SOMERSET PLACE

Gas
Works

Royal Nurseries

112.   Initially the GWR main line through stations had only one platform, in this case on the south side. (This also applied at Reading and Taunton). The opening date is often quoted as 4th June 1841, but an official notice in *The Railway Times* stated 1st June 1840. However, trains stopped here from 1st May 1839, although there was no platform. A clause in the original Act precluded the GWR from constructing any "Station or Depot within three miles of Eton College". But the GWR announced that "the trains will of course convey any passengers who may want to travel to or from Slough, and the Directors regret they are not at liberty to provide the ordinary conveniences of a station". (British Rail)

113.   A broad gauge 4-2-2 of the "Rover" class approaches the station from the London direction. It seems that the rail for broad gauge trains to the cattle dock was little used, but the one on the other siding had some limited use. (LPC/NRM)

114.   A slipped portion of a train is beginning its steady deceleration before stopping in the station and is probably destined for Windsor. Steam heating was cut off at this point. The first such slipping on the GWR took place here in November 1858. The last on the former system was in September 1960. The Iron Works is on the right. (British Rail)

115.   The 1.15pm Paddington to Falmouth train was hauled by 4-2-2 no. 3015 on 18th June 1900, when it ran into the rear of the 1.5pm Paddington to Windsor at about 25mph. Five died. The latter service ran non-stop subsequent to the accident. (LPC/NRM)

116.   The south elevation was featured on a postcard circulating in the late 1920s. Two General buses are on the right. Nearest is an "S" type on route 162 to Leatherhead. No parking problems in those days! The building dates from 1886 and was still in use over a century later. (Lens of Sutton)

117.   The west end of the station had a dock siding (diverging on the left), a centre through road between the relief lines, a short bay line (with platforms both sides), the two main lines and a longer bay, which is occupied by a coach probably bound for Windsor. The centre road was classified as a siding and was removed in October 1958. (Lens of Sutton)

118.   No. 5082 *Swordfish* of the "Castle" class runs through with an up express on 30th June 1951 and nearly obscures an important announcement. Horlicks Malted Milk Company was one of 13 firms with private sidings at Slough. (N.W.Sprinks)

119. The up "Pembroke Coast Express" was derailed west of the station on 1st May 1959, injuring six. The damaged restaurant car was photographed the next day near East Box. This had 59 levers and was in use until 14th October 1963, at the end of platforms 3 and 4. A panel box west of the station took over the area. (F.Hornby)

120. Recently transferred from the Eastern Region, no. 31230 passes through platform 3 on 28th May 1975 with the 08.08 Hereford to Paddington. The space in the foreground was near the camera in picture no. 112. Local freight traffic ceased on 27th July 1975, but passengers are still conveyed in vast numbers at this busy location. (G.Gillham)

MP Middleton Press

Easebourne Lane, Midhurst, W Sussex. GU29 9AZ Tel: 01730 813169 Fax: 01730 812601
*If books are not available from your local transport stockist, order direct with cheque,
Visa or Mastercard, post free UK.*

BRANCH LINES
Branch Line to Allhallows
Branch Line to Alton
Branch Lines around Ascot
Branch Line to Ashburton
Branch Lines around Bodmin
Branch Line to Bude
Branch Lines around Canterbury
Branch Lines around Chard & Yeovil
Branch Line to Cheddar
Branch Lines around Cromer
Branch Lines of East London
Branch Lines to Effingham Junction
Branch Lines around Exmouth
Branch Line to Fairford
Branch Lines around Gosport
Branch Line to Hawkhurst
Branch Line to Hayling
Branch Lines to Horsham
Branch Lines around Huntingdon
Branch Line to Kingswear
Branch Lines to Launceston & Princetown
Branch Lines to Longmoor
Branch Line to Looe
Branch Line to Lyme Regis
Branch Lines around March
Branch Lines around Midhurst
Branch Line to Minehead
Branch Line to Moretonhampstead
Branch Lines to Newport (IOW)
Branch Line to Padstow
Branch Lines around Plymouth
Branch Lines to Seaton and Sidmouth
Branch Line to Selsey
Branch Lines around Sheerness
Branch Line to Shrewsbury
Branch Line to Swanage *updated*
Branch Line to Tenterden
Branch Lines to Torrington
Branch Line to Tunbridge Wells
Branch Line to Upwell
Branch Lines around Weymouth
Branch Lines around Wimborne
Branch Lines around Wisbech

NARROW GAUGE BRANCH LINES
Branch Line to Lynton
Branch Lines around Portmadoc 1923-46
Branch Lines around Porthmadog 1954-94
Branch Line to Southwold
Two-Foot Gauge Survivors
Romneyrail
Vivarais Narrow Gauge

SOUTH COAST RAILWAYS
Ashford to Dover
Bournemouth to Weymouth
Brighton to Eastbourne
Brighton to Worthing
Chichester to Portsmouth
Dover to Ramsgate
Eastbourne to Hastings
Hastings to Ashford
Portsmouth to Southampton
Southampton to Bournemouth
Worthing to Chichester

SOUTHERN MAIN LINES
Basingstoke to Salisbury
Bromley South to Rochester
Crawley to Littlehampton
Dartford to Sittingbourne
East Croydon to Three Bridges
Epsom to Horsham

Exeter to Barnstaple
Exeter to Tavistock
Faversham to Dover
London Bridge to East Croydon
Orpington to Tonbridge
Tonbridge to Hastings
Salisbury to Yeovil
Swanley to Ashford
Tavistock to Plymouth
Victoria to East Croydon
Waterloo to Windsor
Waterloo to Woking
Woking to Portsmouth
Woking to Southampton
Yeovil to Exeter

EASTERN MAIN LINES
Fenchurch Street to Barking
Ipswich to Saxmundham
Liverpool Street to Ilford

WESTERN MAIN LINES
Ealing to Slough
Paddington to Ealing

COUNTRY RAILWAY ROUTES
Andover to Southampton
Bath Green Park to Bristol
Bath to Evercreech Junction
Bournemouth to Evercreech Jn.
Cheltenham to Andover
Croydon to East Grinstead
Didcot to Winchester
East Kent Light Railway
Fareham to Salisbury
Frome to Bristol
Guildford to Redhill
Porthmadog to Blaenau
Reading to Basingstoke
Reading to Guildford
Redhill to Ashford
Salisbury to Westbury
Stratford upon Avon to Cheltenham
Strood to Paddock Wood
Taunton to Barnstaple
Wenford Bridge to Fowey
Westbury to Bath
Woking to Alton
Yeovil to Dorchester

GREAT RAILWAY ERAS
Ashford from Steam to Eurostar
Clapham Junction 50 years of change
Festiniog in the Fifties
Festiniog in the Sixties
Isle of Wight Lines 50 years of change
Railways to Victory 1944-46
SECR Centenary album
Talyllyn 50 years of change
Yeovil 50 years of change

LONDON SUBURBAN RAILWAYS
Caterham and Tattenham Corner
Charing Cross to Dartford
Clapham Jn. to Beckenham Jn.
East London Line
Finsbury Park to Alexandra Palace
Kingston and Hounslow Loops
Lewisham to Dartford
Lines around Wimbledon
London Bridge to Addiscombe
Mitcham Junction Lines
North London Line
South London Line

West Croydon to Epsom
West London Line
Willesden Junction to Richmond
Wimbledon to Epsom

STEAMING THROUGH
Steaming through Cornwall
Steaming through Kent
Steaming through West Hants
Steaming through West Sussex

TRAMWAY CLASSICS
Aldgate & Stepney Tramways
Barnet & Finchley Tramways
Bath Tramways
Bournemouth & Poole Tramways
Brighton's Tramways
Camberwell & W.Norwood Tramwa
Clapham & Streatham Tramways
Dover's Tramways
East Ham & West Ham Tramways
Edgware and Willesden Tramways
Eltham & Woolwich Tramways
Embankment & Waterloo Tramways
Enfield & Wood Green Tramways
Exeter & Taunton Tramways
Gosport & Horndean Tramways
Greenwich & Dartford Tramways
Hammersmith & Hounslow Tramwa
Hampstead & Highgate Tramways
Hastings Tramways
Holborn & Finsbury Tramways
Ilford & Barking Tramways
Kingston & Wimbledon Tramways
Lewisham & Catford Tramways
Liverpool Tramways 1. Eastern Routes
Liverpool Tramways 2. Southern Routes
Maidstone & Chatham Tramways
North Kent Tramways
Norwich Tramways
Portsmouth's Tramways
Reading Tramways
Seaton & Eastbourne Tramways
Shepherds Bush & Uxbridge Tramw
Southampton Tramways
Southend-on-sea Tramways
Southwark & Deptford Tramways
Stamford Hill Tramways
Twickenham & Kingston Tramways
Victoria & Lambeth Tramways
Waltham Cross & Edmonton Tramw
Walthamstow & Leyton Tramways
Wandsworth & Battersea Tramways

TROLLEYBUS CLASSICS
Croydon Trolleybuses
Bournemouth Trolleybuses
Hastings Trolleybuses
Maidstone Trolleybuses
Reading Trolleybuses
Woolwich & Dartford Trolleybuses

WATERWAY ALBUMS
Kent and East Sussex Waterways
London to Portsmouth Waterway
West Sussex Waterways

MILITARY BOOKS
Battle over Portsmouth
Battle over Sussex 1940
Blitz over Sussex 1941-42
Bombers over Sussex 1943-45
Bognor at War
Military Defence of West Sussex
Secret Sussex Resistance
Sussex Home Guard

OTHER RAILWAY BOOKS
Garraway Father & Son
Index to all Middleton Press stations
Industrial Railways of the South-Eas
South Eastern & Chatham Railways
London Chatham & Dover Railway
War on the Line (SR 1939-45)